FOOD AND FEASTS

Stewart Ross

W
HODDER
Wayland

an imprint of Hodder Children's Books

ANCIENT EGYPT
Family Life
Food and Feasts
Pharaohs
Temples, Tombs and Pyramids

© 2001 White-Thomson Publishing Ltd

Produced for Hodder Wayland by
White-Thomson Publishing Ltd
2/3 St Andrew's Place
Lewes BN7 1UP

Editor: Liz Gogerly
Design: Stonecastle Graphics Ltd
Picture research: Shelley Noronha at
  Glass Onion Pictures
Consultant: Dr. J. Fletcher
Proofreader: Alison Cooper
Artwork: John Yates
Map artwork: Peter Bull

Published in Great Britain in 2001 by Hodder Wayland,
an imprint of Hodder Children's Books.
This paperback edition published in 2001.

All rights reserved. No part of this publication may be reproduced, stored in a retrieval system, or transmitted, in any form or by any means without the prior written permission of the publisher, nor be otherwise circulated in any form of binding or cover other than that in which it is published and without a similar condition being imposed on the subsequent purchaser.

The right of Stewart Ross to be identified as the author has been asserted by him in accordance with the Copyright, Designs and Patents Act, 1988.

Picture acknowledgements
The publisher would like to thank the following for their kind permission to use their pictures:
AKG, London (contents), 5, 7, 13, 15, 16, 17, 20, 21, 23, 24, 28, 34, 36, 37, 40, 41 (bottom); **Art Archive** 4, 6, 11, 12, 32, 39, 42; **Peter Clayton** 18, 25; **Dennis Day** 14, 22, 33, 35, 43; **Werner Forman** 9, 10, 30, 38; **Hodder Wayland Picture Library** 27, 29/ © British Museum 41 (top), 44, 45; **Michael Holford** (cover), 26.

Please note that the language of the quotations in this book has been translated in a way to make it accessible to younger readers. The precise date of each quotation is generally not known.

British Library Cataloguing in Publication Data
Ross, Stewart
  Food & Feasts. - (Ancient Egypt)
  1. Food habits - Egypt - History - Juvenile literature
  2. Fasts and Feasts - Egypt - History - Juvenile literature
  3. Egypt - Social life and customs - To 332 B.C. -
  Juvenile literature
  I. Title
  932

ISBN 0 7502 3373 7

Printed and bound in Italy
by Eurografica S.p.a.

Hodder Children's Books
A division of Hodder Headline Limited
338 Euston Road
London NW1 3BH

CONTENTS

Chapter 1
Everything Ready! 4

Chapter 2
The Land of the Nile 8

Chapter 3
Trading for Food 18

Chapter 4
Meal Time 24

Chapter 5
Festivals and Feasts 32

Chapter 6
Uncovering Ancient Egypt 42

Glossary 46

Time Line 47

Further Information 47

Index 48

BRIGHTON & HOVE COUNCIL	
02551834	
Cypher	28.03.02
932 JN	£3.08
	651506

Food and Feasts

1 Everything Ready!

Peseshet glanced around to make sure she was alone. Not a soul. With a sigh of relief, she sank down in the shade of her favourite sycamore. Peseshet leaned back against its ancient trunk and shut her eyes. The heavy scent of lotus blossom closed around her.

The old servant woman was exhausted. She had been on her feet all day, helping to prepare for the great banquet they were holding at the villa that evening. At last, now her mistress was taking a nap, she was free to slip away into the garden for a rest.

Sack of idleness!

'Pese-shet! Where are you, sack of idleness?' Atet's voice cut through the hot air like an arrow.

Peseshet opened her eyes. Oh no! 'Here, mistress!', she cried, scrambling to her feet and hurrying back to the house to carry on with the preparations for the feast.

Milk for the mistress – Queen Ashayet, wife of King Mentuhotep II, is offered a drink of milk by a servant. The servant behind her holds a fan that is also used to get rid of flies.

Everything Ready!

The nineteen-year-old Atet was the second wife of the elderly nomarch Dagi and mistress of his household. She was a handsome but stern-faced young woman who had recently given birth to her first child. This evening's banquet was in honour of Hathor, the goddess of love, beauty and childbirth. Never kind at the best of times, this afternoon Atet was nervous about the party and in a foul mood.

Fresh pigeon

'Where were you, servant?' demanded Atet, glaring at Peseshet through her heavily made-up eyes.

Peseshet thought fast. 'Just checking that everything was tidy in the garden, noble mistress,' she replied, bowing almost to the floor.

Atet snorted. 'Right. Straight to the kitchens. Check that everything is ready, then report back to me.'

Peseshet shuffled off to the kitchens at the other end of the villa. First she checked the storeroom. Everything seemed in place. Then she chatted with the cooks and was told that all the dishes – yes, including the roasted pigeon – would be cooked and served just as the mistress wanted.

As well as holding banquets, many women made offerings in honour of the goddess Hathor. In this painting, Queen Nefertari offers two precious vases to the horn-headed goddess.

'Don't judge people by their wealth but by their behaviour.'

From the *Wisdoms of Merikare*, a king of the Tenth Dynasty.

Food and Feasts

Rehearsal time

Atet was still not satisfied. Had Peseshet checked all the rooms? No? What use was a chief servant who didn't do her job? The old woman set off again, making sure everywhere the guests might go was spotlessly clean. She paid particular attention to the great hall where the stool and tables had been arranged for the banquet.

Next, she was sent to see that the musicians, dancers and other entertainers had turned up. She found them practising in the courtyard near the main gate.

Family feast – a father (seated), surrounded by his wife, son and servants, prepares to tuck into a meal of bread and meat on an offering table.

Charming!

At last, Atet seemed happy with the preparations. But Peseshet's work was still not done. She now had to supervise the younger servants who were helping their mistress get herself ready.

First Atet was washed with jugs of clean water, then rubbed with scented oils and helped into her clothes. She put on a long white dress, decorated with pleats and trimmed with elaborate fringes that had been made specially for the occasion. When Atet was satisfied with how she looked, Peseshet brought out the best wig and fitted it over her mistress' shaved head. 'Charming, your ladyship!' said Peseshet politely.

Atet looked at her in surprise. 'Of course! Did you think I wouldn't be?'

Everything Ready!

Hold still, please! A servant girl adjusts the collars and jewellery of three ladies preparing for a feast.

Of course!

After the wig, the jewellery. Peseshet was the only servant allowed to touch it. Very carefully she brought out a magnificent gold collar, inlaid with turquoise, and fixed it round her mistress' neck. Then came the rings, armlets and earrings, all blazing with precious minerals.

Finally, the make-up: heavy black kohl for the eyes, and red ochre for the lips and cheeks. When all was finished, Atet told Peseshet to go and fetch her husband. 'What do you think?' she asked when the balding Dagi appeared.

'Charming!' he smiled. 'Quite charming!'

'Of course,' nodded Atet. 'Now everything is ready for tonight's feast.'

"When she opens her eyes, she makes me young again.'
From a New Kingdom love poem.

7

Food and Feasts

2 The Land of the Nile

Dagi and his household lived almost 3,400 years ago, during the reign of Amenhotep III (about 1390–1352 BC). Historians divide the history of ancient Egypt into four eras: the Old Kingdom (about 2690–2180 BC), the Middle Kingdom (about 2055–1650 BC), the New Kingdom (about 1550–1070 BC) and the Late Period (about 747–332 BC). 'Intermediate Periods' of war and uncertainty divided these eras.

The long reign of Amenhotep III, during the New Kingdom, saw Egypt at its most magnificent. It was ruler of a large empire and its people lived in peace and prosperity. Dagi, Atet and Peseshet were fortunate to have lived at such a time.

God-like kings

The king was by far the most important person in Egypt. He was more than an all-powerful ruler. The land was his and he

A map of ancient Egypt during the New Kingdom period.

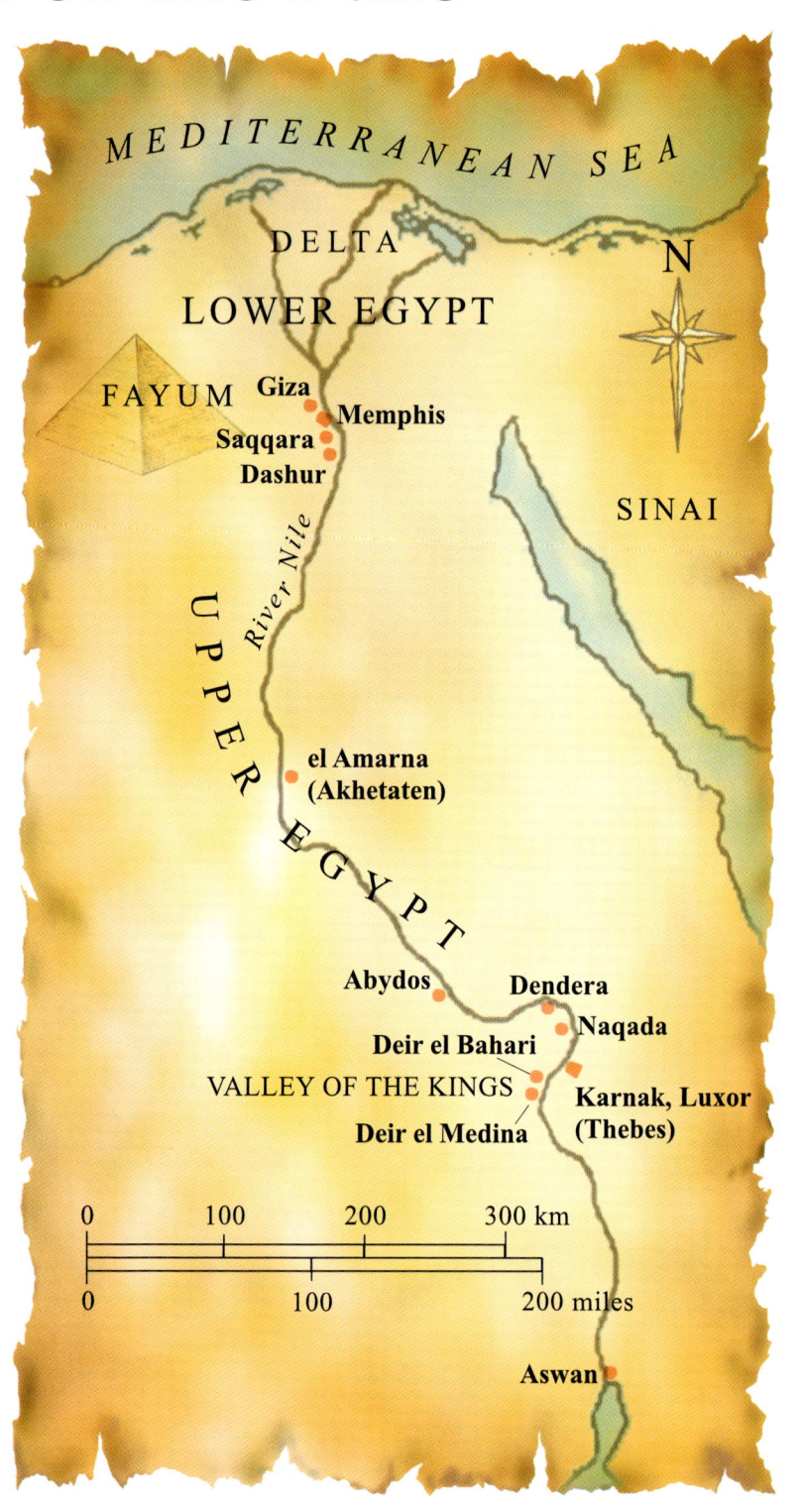

The Land of the Nile

supervised everything that went on, from worship to irrigation. He was also worshipped as semi-divine. Indeed, some early kings were gods in their own lifetimes. The Egyptians believed that all their kings became gods after they died.

The king's god-like position was vital to ancient Egypt's survival. The Egyptians believed there was a constant struggle in the universe between order (or 'ma'at') and chaos (or 'izfet'). Only the gods could preserve order in the world. The semi-divine king had the power to keep the gods on his side and so maintain order.

A procession bearing offerings for the annual festival of Opet is shown on this relief from Amenhotep III's column in the temple in Luxor.

Pharaohs and dynasties

Kings had many names, such as 'Son of Re'(the sun god) and 'Living Horus'. Kings of the New Kingdom were also called 'Pharaoh'. Rather than call some rulers 'king' and others 'pharaoh', it is simpler to call them all 'king'.

Between 3150 and 332 BC, thirty-one families ruled Egypt in succession. Each family is known as a Dynasty. Amenhotep III was the ninth ruler of the Eighteenth Dynasty (often written 'Dynasty XVIII') which lasted from about 1550 to 1295 BC.

> *'He who rebels against the king would pull down Heaven.'*
>
> From the *Wisdoms of Merikare*, a king of the Tenth Dynasty.

Food and Feasts

Viziers and nomarchs

The king's most important helper was the vizier, a sort of prime minister. Beneath him were the high priests and forty-two nomarchs (like Dagi in chapter one). Each nomarch was in charge of a province, or 'nome'. During the Old Kingdom the nomarchs became very powerful, acting like hereditary lords of their provinces. Other important officials were scribes (clerks skilled at writing) and army officers.

The land of little change

Ancient Egyptian civilization changed remarkably little over its 3,000-year history. This was partly because of its obsession with order. Furthermore, natural barriers – desert and sea – cut Egypt off from other early civilizations. Finally, the civilization followed the regular rhythms of the river Nile. As the river rarely changed its behaviour, neither did the people who depended on it –

The Scribe of Amenophis II hunts gazelles and other desert animals from high up on his chariot.

the food people ate and the festivals held in honour of their gods changed little over ancient Egypt's long and fascinating history.

Nevertheless, some things did change. For example, the population of the New Kingdom (about three million) was double that of the Old Kingdom. Religious practices, too, changed from one era to the next.

A religious world

Religion was not part of Egyptian civilization – it *was* Egyptian civilization. Just as modern Western civilization looks to science to explain the world, so the Egyptians looked to their many deities. They believed the gods and goddesses affected their daily lives at every turn. Everything they did, said or thought had a religious aspect. The sun, for example, was a display of the sun god Re. Similarly, Atet knew she had to thank Hathor for the safe delivery of her child. If she did not, then the goddess probably would not allow her to have another baby. Feasts or offerings were the usual way of honouring a god.

Coffin code: this picture, found on a coffin, shows the priest (wearing a leopard skin) offering gifts to the god Osiris. As Osiris was the ruler of the Underworld, it was vital that the dead were well prepared to please him.

'Re, the mightiest of the gods, lived on earth as a mortal pharaoh surrounded by human beings that he had created.'

From *The Eye of Re* found in the tomb of King Seti I.

Food and Feasts

The river of life

Egypt is a largely barren land of desert and rocky mountains. The exception is the fertile strip on either side of the river Nile. The river flows from south to north across the entire country. Where it enters the Mediterranean, it fans out into a delta of dozens of smaller channels.

Without the Nile there could have been no ancient Egyptian civilization. Its waters gave life to people, animals and crops. Not surprisingly, it was associated with many deities. Osiris arranged the annual flood and taught people how to farm the rich riverbank soil. The chubby Hapi represented the river's goodness.

Three seasons

The Egyptian year closely followed the Nile's three phases. Between February and June, when there was no rain in the East African Highlands, the river ran low and Egypt was in drought. This was the time of harvest.

How high? How fast? The pool at Dendera with the flight of steps that acted as a 'Nilometer' – the height of the Nile was measured in steps covered by the waters. The rate of the river's rise or fall could also be measured.

The Land of the Nile

Fishermen at work with their net in a bed of papyrus reeds.

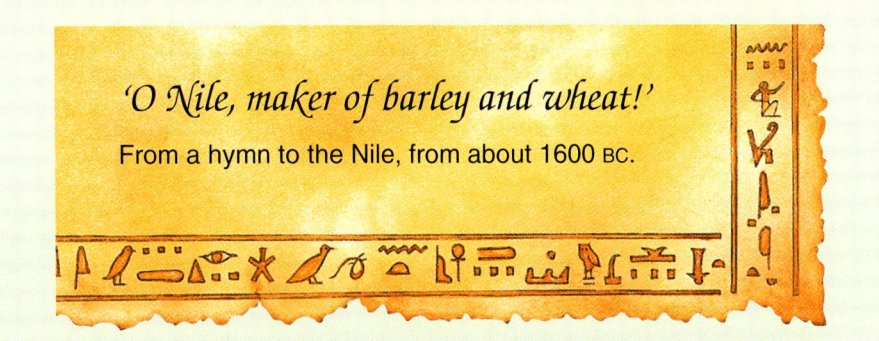

When the rains came, usually in June, the river rose and flooded the fields along its banks. Occasionally, it rose even higher, washing away whole villages. If it failed to rise to its normal height, the harvest was poor and famine threatened.

As the river receded after July, farmers tried to conserve the floodwater in canals and reservoirs. Finally, the farmland was marked out again and planted with new crops.

Egypt's bounty

The Nile gave Egypt more than just water. Mud from the river bank was used for pottery. People fashioned water jugs, large storage vessels, cups and dishes from the Nile's red mud. It was also a rich food source – fish from the Nile made a nutritious and tasty meal. The Egyptians learned to use the dense papyrus reeds that grew along the river banks. They wove the stalks into household objects, such as mats and baskets, which could be used to carry and store provisions. Finally, the Nile was a central highway, linking the different regions of a kingdom over 1,000 kilometres long.

'O Nile, maker of barley and wheat!'
From a hymn to the Nile, from about 1600 BC.

Food and Feasts

Farmers and labourers

We cannot tell exactly where most Egyptians lived. Ordinary families dwelt in small houses of mud brick that have long since disappeared. It seems certain that the majority were gathered in villages. In the New Kingdom only about 10 per cent of the population lived in towns or cities. These included most of the upper-class families, like Dagi's.

For eight or nine months of the year the peasants worked in the fields. However, agricultural land was under water during the flood season, freeing labourers for other work. As far as we know, this was the time when thousands of them worked on royal building projects, such as a temple or pyramid.

Careful organization

Egypt was very tightly organized. Each year water channels and storage basins were cleared or re-dug. Fields were laid out, crops gathered and stored, and taxes collected. As no farmer or group of farmers could do this on their own, it was organized by royal officials.

Dagi and the other nomarchs, helped by scribes and lesser officials, supervised the work. One of their tasks was to plan how much land would be cultivated each year. They then collected taxes (in the form of produce) accordingly. After a heavy flood, for example, crops were

Modern-day irrigation of fields beside the Nile. The scene would probably not have looked very different in the time of the pharaohs.

planted over a wider area than normal, and more food was gathered into the royal storehouses.

Rope-stretchers

The Egyptians distinguished between 'red land' and 'black land'. Red land was the desert, where no crops grew. Black land was the soil beside the Nile where fresh layers of rich mud were deposited each year. On this fertile land grew the crops that provided Egypt with most of its wealth.

The flood swept away all boundary markers. So, as soon as the waters had receded, surveyors plotted out the fields again. They were known as 'rope-stretchers' because they measured areas with long pieces of rope. At the same time, teams of diggers reconstructed the irrigation system.

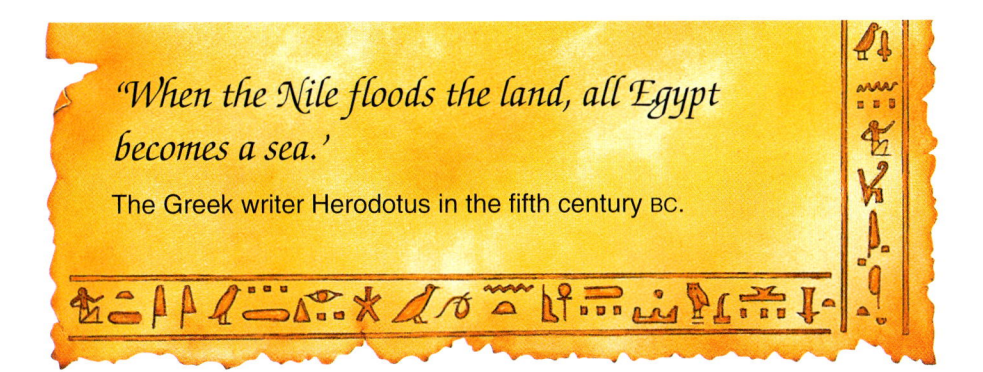

A royal official (centre) measures a field with a length of rope. Because markings were washed away in the annual flood, fields had to be mapped out again each year.

'When the Nile floods the land, all Egypt becomes a sea.'
The Greek writer Herodotus in the fifth century BC.

Food and Feasts

The fruits of the earth

The country's principal crops were a type of wheat (emmer-wheat) and barley. These were made into several different types of bread and cakes. Barley was also used to make beer. Vegetables included beans, lentils, leeks, onions and lettuces.

Nile water irrigated orchards situated above the area normally flooded by the river. Here grew all kinds of fruits, such as melons, figs, dates and pomegranates. The Egyptians were fond of herbs, too, and used them in medicines and to liven up their food. Vines provided grapes for eating or making into wine. Oil, needed for cooking, burning in lamps and cosmetics, was extracted from castor-oil plants, sesame seeds and flax.

Winnowing the threshed grain. Using wooden scoops, the workers throw the grain and chaff into the air. The light chaff is blown away and the heavy grain, needed for making bread, falls to the ground.

Harvest

Farmers prepared the soil for planting with a kind of short-handled hoe. This was back-breaking work. When the crop was ripe, it was cut down with a sickle and carried in bundles to an area of hard, dry ground for threshing. It is likely that women and children lent a hand in the fields at this time.

Threshing involved beating the grain with a stick (flail). This broke the hard grain from its light casing (chaff). To separate the grain from the chaff it was winnowed – pitched into the air on a windy day so that the chaff blew away and the heavy grain fell to the floor.

The riches of Egypt: fruits, fowl and bread piled high for a funeral feast.

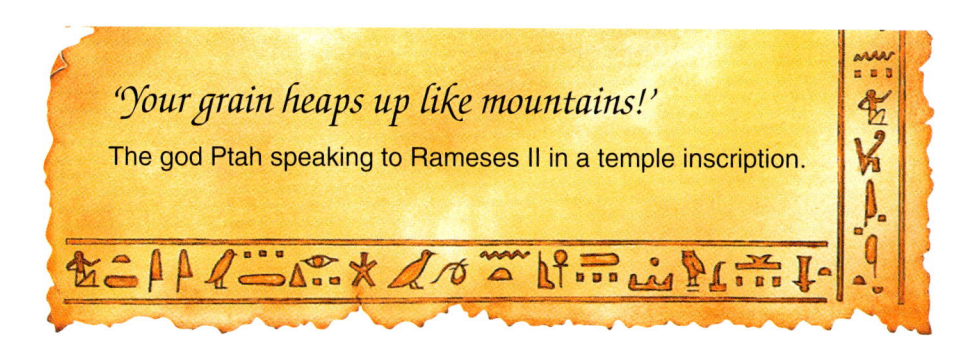

Fish, beasts and birds

The diet of cereals and vegetables was varied with fish from the river and the irrigation canals. Nile perch was a popular catch. Villagers kept goats and geese from which they obtained milk, wool, eggs and meat. Often temples would keep their own herds of cattle. Sheep and pigs were less common. Evidence suggests that meat from these animals was normally eaten mainly by wealthy people.

The Egyptians were keen hunters. They trapped birds such as ducks and geese in nets. Skilled hunters could also hit flying birds with heavy throwing sticks.

'Your grain heaps up like mountains!'
The god Ptah speaking to Rameses II in a temple inscription.

Food and Feasts

3 Trading for Food

Like many wealthy Egyptians during the New Kingdom, the family of nomarch Dagi enjoyed the fruits of foreign trade. The rich wine he served at his banquet was imported from Palestine.

Egypt usually produced more food than was needed to feed its population, but it was always short of wood for building and for use in cooking. From early times, therefore, royal merchants sailed to the eastern Mediterranean to exchange grain for timber. Later, with the growth of the Egyptian empire, trade expanded to include a wide range of goods and materials.

A nation of boat builders

Because ancient Egypt was a river civilization, its people were skilled boat builders. The first crafts were made of bundles of reeds. Later, two important discoveries improved boat building. One was the sail, which allowed boats to move swiftly upstream, carried by winds blowing off the Mediterranean. The second was using wood to build boats and ships.

Wooden ships were much larger than those made of reeds. Some were over 40 metres long. They were driven by oars as well as a square sail, and steered by a paddle at the stern. Vessels like these were able to sail in the rough waters of the Mediterranean, and enabled the Egyptians to trade for food far beyond their native shore.

Sailing down the Nile. When boats sailed north the strong current of the Nile meant there was no need for sails. Boats sailing south needed wind and the sails up.

Across the Mediterranean

Egypt's most important trade was with the lands of Palestine, Canaan and Phoenicia at the eastern end of the Mediterranean. The ancient port of Byblos in Phoenicia was one of Egypt's first trading partners.

Egyptians crossed the sea with cargoes of grain, cloth, papyrus, gold and gemstones. These were exchanged for timber and luxury goods such as wines, perfumes and oils. When metal technology developed, the Egyptians also needed tin and copper to make bronze. At the end of the New Kingdom, when iron was first employed, that metal too was imported.

A map showing the major trade routes and goods traded by the Egyptians during the New Kingdom.

Food and Feasts

In the name of the king

Because the king was all-powerful, all trade was carried out in his name. Foreign traders visiting Egypt were seen as bringing gifts for the king and receiving goods from him in return. The king also collected a heavy duty on all goods brought into Egypt.

The king had a network of royal servants, like modern ambassadors, in many different countries. Their task was to look after Egypt's interests, which included acquiring goods needed at home. The wealthier temples also had foreign agents. The great temple of Amun even ran a fleet of over eighty trading vessels.

Monument to the mightiest female king of all – Hatshepsut's magnificent temple cut from solid rock at Deir el Bahari. The temple was built as a place where Hatshepsut could be worshipped after her death.

South to Punt

One of Egypt's most famous trading voyages took place during the reign of Queen Hatshepsut in the fifteenth century BC. She sent three ships on a route rarely used by Egyptian sailors. They sailed south down the Red Sea to the land of Punt. This was probably near modern Somalia, on the edge of the Indian Ocean. The aim of the voyage was to trade directly with East Africa.

'As the reign of Rameses the Great continued, more and more lands came under his control until he was the most powerful ruler on earth.'
From *The Princess and the Demon*, from about 200 BC.

According to the carvings on the queen's temple at Deir el Bahari, near Thebes, the voyage was a great success. Egyptian goods were exchanged for cargoes of exotic luxuries – great elephant tusks, beautiful animal skins, ebony, myrrh and frankincense.

Filling the hold – workers empty their sacks of grain into a boat. Water transport was by far the easiest way to carry heavy loads in ancient Egypt.

Food from taxes

Under the warrior kings of the New Kingdom, Egypt's power spread south into Nubia (Sudan), west into Libya and north-east to the River Euphrates. The conquered lands in the south were ruled as part of Egypt and forced to pay high taxes. Taxation was paid in food, wood, minerals and slaves. These were shipped to Egypt at the taxpayers' expense. Several luxury items and foodstuffs in Dagi's villa had come to Egypt as taxes.

The people of Palestine, Syria and Phoenicia governed themselves but they had to swear not to rebel. If they broke their word or refused to pay taxes, the Egyptian army was sent to sort them out.

Food and Feasts

Donkeys in the desert

Not all Egyptian trade was done by water. Journeys to Nubia and the Sudan, for example, were partly overland because the Nile's cataracts (rapids) stopped boats sailing much beyond the city of Elephantine. Traders also went overland to Libya and across the Sinai desert to Palestine. As there were no roads, a reliable guide was essential.

Merchants travelled on foot, moving from oasis to oasis across the desert with a caravan of donkeys. It was slow going – on an average day they went no more than 19 kilometres. The trek south to the Sudan was known as the 'Forty Days' route because that was how long it took.

Nubia

The frontier with Nubia, to the south-east of the first cataract, saw much fighting over the centuries. To prevent Nubian raids, the Egyptians gradually extended their frontier south from cataract to cataract.

The Egyptians were interested in Nubia not just for security reasons. The land provided two valuable

The vast sands of the Sahara Desert that lie beyond the narrow strip of fertile land beside the Nile.

commodities: gold and slaves. It was also linked with the regions supplying luxuries such as ivory, scented woods, leopard skins and ostrich feathers. These were either traded for Egyptian produce or, in the New Kingdom, collected as tribute from the conquered people.

Slaves

Egypt's slaves were foreigners who had been bought, captured or collected as tribute. Peseshet, for example, was born in Nubia. As a young girl she was handed over to Egyptian officials and given to the king. He made a present of her to Dagi's father.

Household servants, who could be foreign or Egyptian, could live quite comfortably. A few learned to read and write and rose to important positions. However, most servants remained in the service of their masters and mistresses. Images of servants laden with food are seen throughout ancient Egyptian art.

Royal reward: a golden plate given by the warrior king Thutmose III to General Djehuty who captured the city of Joppa in Palestine.

'Then the King of Nubia, far away to the south, sent an ambassador to Thebes to meet with the Pharaoh.'

From the New Kingdom folk tale *Se-Osiris*, from about the twelfth century BC.

Food and Feasts

4 Meal Time

Just as the land of Egypt belonged to the king, so its produce was his also. Farmers kept part of their crops for immediate needs and handed over the rest to temples and royal officers. Because of the king's god-like status and because the penalties for non-payment were harsh, these taxes were normally paid without grumbling. One of Dagi's tasks was to collect the produce due to the king from his nome.

Grain, goods and valuable materials were kept in royal storehouses. They were issued as wages to royal servants and workers on building projects.

A healthy diet – the Egyptian diet seems to have been well balanced, with plenty of fresh fruit and vegetables to go with the meat and bread.

Diet

Compared with the rather fatty and stodgy foods we eat, the diet of most ancient Egyptians was healthy. People ate little meat or dairy produce. Instead, the basis of every meal was bread, a healthy source of energy. Fish was a valuable source of protein. None of their food was processed or treated with artificial preservatives, colouring or flavouring. Minerals and vitamins came from fresh fruits and vegetables.

That said, Egyptians didn't eat healthily by choice, and eating a balanced diet was a matter of chance. And, as with any culture, the poor often went hungry, and when the Nile floods failed they faced serious starvation.

Preserving food

Although preserving food was a problem, it was easier in Egypt than in lands with wetter climates. Families kept dry foods, such as grain and flour, in large pottery jars. As there was no refrigeration, other foods had to be dried, salted, pickled or smoked before storage. Even then, flies and vermin were a constant problem. Certain foods, such as most fruits, had to be eaten fresh.

Meat and fish were often preserved by salting or smoking. Salting involved leaving the cleaned flesh soaking in salt water for a long time then hanging it up to dry. Smoking meant hanging the meat over a smoky fire. This gave it a pleasant woody flavour.

Mud from the river Nile was often turned on a wheel and made into pottery, such as this jug.

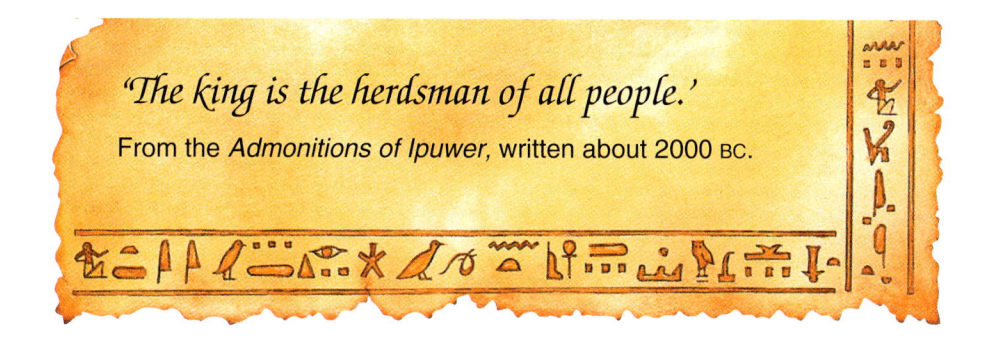

'The king is the herdsman of all people.'
From the *Admonitions of Ipuwer*, written about 2000 BC.

Food and Feasts

Bread

Bread was the staple food of ancient Egypt and they had more than a dozen names for it. Each household did its own baking. First, the grains of wheat or barley were ground up to produce flour. This was mixed with water, then kneaded (massaged) to make dough.

The dough was divided into loaves which were baked in a clay vessel over an open fire. The Egyptians were the first to bake bread in this way. They also discovered how to make dough rise by adding yeast. Unleavened bread (made without yeast) was quite hard and flat. Seeds, honey, butter and other flavourings cheered up the taste of the ordinary loaf.

Water

The Nile kept Egypt alive. Apart from wells and isolated oases in the desert, it was the country's only source of water for drinking, cooking and washing. Each morning thousands of servants, slaves and housewives trudged down to the river to collect water in large pottery jars.

Butchers, bakers and brewers at work (left to right). These delightful wooden models were made to accompany a dead person into the afterlife, so that they would not go hungry there.

Meal Time

> *'I have never committed the sin of grabbing bread from a child.'*
>
> From the *Book of the Dead*, written at the end of the New Kingdom.

Compared with the clean water we draw from taps, Nile water was brown and dirty. It might also carry diseases, especially infections of the intestine. Not surprisingly, therefore, the Egyptians enjoyed other drinks. Fruit juices were cool and refreshing. But the most popular drink with all ages was beer. It not only tasted good but, because it contained alcohol, it was free from germs.

Beer and brewing

Beer was quick and easy to make. It was also a useful source of nutrition. All brewing was done at home using grains of barley, barley bread and water. The loaves were broken up and mixed with dried grains of barley. This mixture was placed in a large jar filled with water.

Over a period of days, the mixture fermented to produce beer. When it was ready, the clear liquid was poured off into clean jars leaving the sludge at the bottom. Judging by many paintings, carvings and inscriptions, no Egyptian feast or festival was complete without a large supply of fresh beer.

Ancient bread. Remarkably, Egypt's dry climate has preserved these dense, flat loaves for thousands of years.

Food and Feasts

Wine

Atet served wine as well as beer at her banquet. Wine took longer to make than beer, and grape vines were found only on the estates of the nobility. Special wines were also imported from countries in the eastern Mediterranean (see the map on page 19).

Wine was made by picking ripe grapes. The juice was fermented in open jars, then transferred to smaller jars with stoppers. These jars were carefully labelled with the wine's date, where it was made and which type of grape had been used.

Pots and pans

We know little about how or where ordinary families prepared their meals. Only some people had separate kitchens. Cooking was done over an open fire or in a clay oven. Fires were lit either in a shady spot outside or in the centre of the main downstairs room of the house. As firewood was scarce and lighting a fire in summer made

Wine time – men stamping grapes in a wine press to drive out the juice from which wine will be made. The juice is being collected in the basin on the right, ready to be put into the jars above.

Meal Time

the interior of a house extremely hot, cooking was kept to a minimum. Utensils were made of pottery turned on a wheel.

Royal palaces and large villas like Atet's had separate kitchen areas. These were equipped with a clay oven and, by the New Kingdom, a wide variety of metal pots and pans.

The daily menu

Most Egyptian homes were run by the mother, helped by her unmarried daughters. They were in charge of all food preparation, including baking and brewing. Only in the largest households was this work done by servants.

Most families ate a basic meal three times a day. The main ingredients were always bread and beer. To this was added fruit (perhaps figs or a melon), raw or boiled vegetables (perhaps beans and onions) and dried fish. The regular meals of a household like Atet's were much more varied. They included different kinds of meat and other dishes prepared with interesting spices and herbs.

A pair of pottery drinking cups made from clay found on the banks of the Nile.

"When Osiris became king, he taught his people how to plant and harvest crops and how to grow vines for wine."
From the traditional tale, *Osiris and Isis*.

Food and Feasts

At home with the ducks

The homes of ordinary people were made of mud brick. Very few have survived, so we only have a rough idea of what they looked like.

They had a flat roof where families slept in hot weather. Downstairs there were one or more rooms with windows (just holes in the wall) high up to let out the smoke and help keep the house cool. Farming families may have used the front part of the house, with their animals, geese and chickens living at the back. Meals were probably eaten in the main front room or outside in the shade. Most people did not have a separate dining room.

A wealthy husband and wife, dressed in their best white clothes, sit close together before an altar table filled with food offerings for the gods.

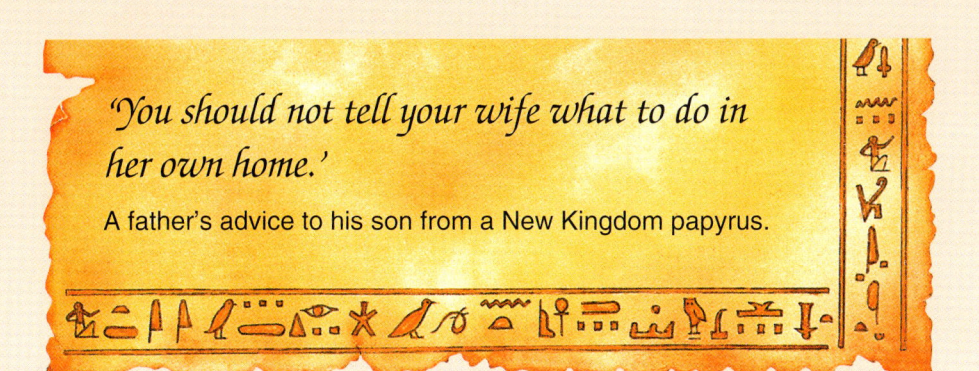

'You should not tell your wife what to do in her own home.'

A father's advice to his son from a New Kingdom papyrus.

Villas

The larger houses, known as villas, were grand buildings of brick and stone. Some had more than twenty main rooms centred around a lofty hall set with columns. They were decorated with coloured tiles and beautiful paintings. Outside there were storerooms, stables and large walled gardens with pools, flowers and trees.

Banquets were held in the main hall, where there was space for entertainment as well as eating. When they did not have guests, the family ate in one of the smaller rooms. Servants and slaves ate in the back rooms, out of sight of their master and mistress.

Furniture

The simplest homes had very little furniture – just a few brick benches, an occasional three or four-legged stool and perhaps a low table.

People usually ate their meals at home sitting on the ground. The wealthy propped themselves up on thick cushions. Poorer families ate off a low table or mat. Their food was served in rough pottery dishes or even on plates of woven reeds. The rich ate off dishes made of fine pottery, silver or gold. As there was no glass, drinking cups were also made of precious metals. Forks and spoons were unknown and everyone ate with their fingers.

Food and Feasts

5 Festivals and Feasts

A nagging worry lurked at the back of the mind of most thinking Egyptians. Their civilization, so strong and impressive, was also very fragile. What if the Nile ceased its annual flood? What if one evening the sun set and never rose again? What if the cycle of the seasons stopped, leaving a world of continual summer or winter? If any of these things happened, ancient Egyptian civilization would vanish for ever.

With our scientific knowledge, we know these fears were largely groundless. But to the Egyptians they were very real. This made ritual – performing special acts over and over again – a key part of their culture.

Music fit for the gods – a priest, shown without his wig, plays his harp before the sun god Re, King of the Gods.

Ritual

The Egyptians believed they had to please the gods to make sure the cycles of life and nature never failed. This led to daily god-pleasing rituals in temples. It also gave rise to much larger annual festivals of god-praising.

King Akhenaten (about 1352–1336 BC) gave religious ritual a new direction. He proclaimed that Aten, the sun disc, was the supreme god. This made some sense – if the sun continued to rise and set, then everything else would probably fall into place. Aten-worship meant setting up lots more altars (each one to feed the god) and worshipping in the open air. The Aten cult was abandoned under Tutankhamun (about 1336–1322 BC).

Festivals and Feasts

'Put on your sacred sandals, go to the temple ... renew the offerings on the altar.'

From the *Wisdoms of Merikare*, a king of the Tenth Dynasty.

Joy and hope

Historians used to think Egyptian culture was rather gloomy. They believed its ever-present fear of chaos was pessimistic. The fact that so many of its monuments were connected with death (the pyramids, for example, are enormous tombs) appeared depressing.

Over the last fifty years or so, this dark view of Egypt has changed. We now see its civilization as optimistic. Tombs mattered because they were a staging post on the way to a new life in a better world. The regular rising of the sun, and the arrival of spring and flooding of the Nile were causes of joy. They were greeted with smiles and, on occasion, spectacular feasts and festivals.

The great pyramids of Giza, built to house the tombs of kings of the Old Kingdom. The pyramids pointed to the sky, the home of Re.

Food and Feasts

Time to celebrate

Broadly speaking, ordinary Egyptians enjoyed two kinds of celebration. Both were religious because life and religion were interwoven. The most common type of celebration concerned individuals and family life. It involved thanking one or more deities for something that had happened, like recovery from illness or the birth of a child. Atet's banquet in chapter one was just this type of celebration, although it was much grander than most families could afford.

The second type of celebration was a public festival. It was usually an annual event, led by priests. Festivals generally involved parading a deity's statue in public. For most people it was also an opportunity for merry-making.

The ancient cow goddess Hathor. Most Egyptian or Egyptian-influenced gods and goddesses were shown as part-human, part-animal.

Horus and Hathor

Over time the personalities and powers of Egypt's many deities changed. Nevertheless, the ancient sky god Horus (meaning 'He Who Is On High') was always respected. He carried the staff of life and was sometimes shown as a falcon. Although Horus carried the staff of life, he could not reproduce without a partner. The one usually associated with him was Hathor. She was the goddess associated with childbirth. She was sometimes shown with cow's horns, symbols of fertility and plenty, or with long curling hair, as she was also known as the goddess of love and beauty.

Festivals and Feasts

The Festival of the Beautiful Embrace

In later times, the union of Horus and Hathor was celebrated in the Festival of the Beautiful Embrace. This fourteen-day festival was a symbol of the creation of all new human life. It took the form of a 'marriage' between the two deities.

The statue of Hathor was taken from its temple at Dendera and placed on a boat called the 'Mistress of Love'. It then proceeded upstream to Horus' temple at Edfu, stopping several times on the way. At Edfu, Horus' statue was brought out to meet Hathor's. Then (the details are not known) the 'beautiful embrace' took place. Like other popular festivals, the religious proceedings were accompanied by entertainment and festivities.

'The gentle goddess Hathor had fallen in love with Horus and went to look for him in the desert.'
From the tale of *Osiris and Isis*.

The statue of Horus, the falcon god, in the temple at Edfu. The kings of ancient Egypt were said to be Horus on earth. A late myth said Horus was the son of Osiris and Isis.

Food and Feasts

The Opet Festival

The greatest festival from the New Kingdom onwards celebrated the river journey of the god Amun from his temple at Karnak to Luxor and back. It was known as the Opet. Amun, sometimes shown with a ram's head, was the god of Thebes in southern Egypt and later became the state god, 'king of the Gods' in the New Kingdom.

Accompanied by singers, dancers, musicians and other entertainers, a procession carrying special boats wound through large crowds to the river. The biggest boat, called Userhat (Powerful Prow) had a ram's head at either end. Once the god's statue was safely aboard, gangs of men hauled Userhat upstream to Luxor. The festival took place in late summer, thanking Amun for the annual flood.

Abydos Festival

All Egyptians knew the myth of the lover-deities, Isis and Osiris. Osiris, Lord of the Earth, was murdered and later cut up into pieces by his wicked brother Seth. Isis, Osiris' heartbroken sister-wife, collected up the bits of his body, brought them to life and had a son (Horus) by him.

The ruins of the mighty temple of Karnak at Thebes. Originally built to honour the god Amun, it contained shrines to several other deities.

Festivals and Feasts

Osiris' severed head was supposed to have been buried at Abydos in Upper Egypt, where a large temple was built in his honour. Many ancient kings were buried there, too, and it became a popular place of pilgrimage. Everyone who could afford it came to the Abydos Festival, when the story of Isis and Osiris was re-created with much drama and pageantry.

Household gods

The Egyptians felt closest to their household gods, Bes and Taweret. Many homes had places set aside for their worship. Bes had a double role: he kept an eye on fertility and childbirth and also warded off evil spirits. To help him with this last task he looked horrific, a sort of lion-headed dwarf holding a knife. Images of Bes and Taweret were often carved on furniture.

Bastet, the cat goddess, had her own festival day, a public holiday that seems to have been enormously popular with Egyptians. The entertainments were provided by the authorities, and towns and villages crowded with singers, dancers and revellers enjoying a rare day off work.

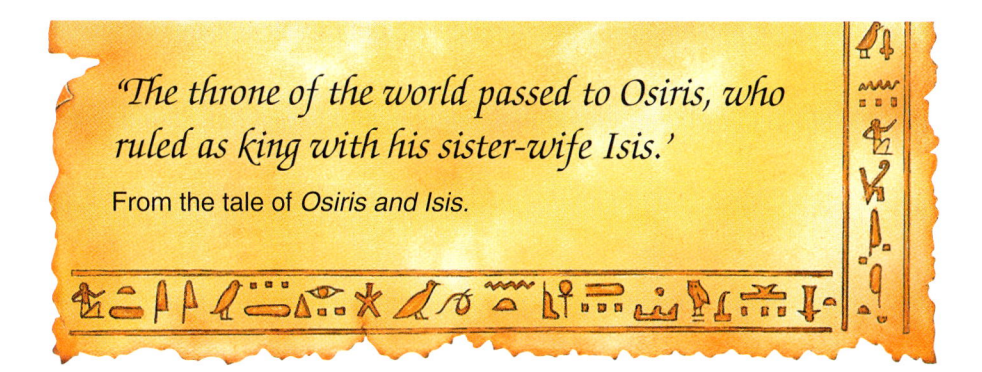

The god Osiris (centre) is flanked by his wife and sister, Isis, and their son Horus. To show they were super-human, kings, like the gods, were allowed to marry their sisters.

'The throne of the world passed to Osiris, who ruled as king with his sister-wife Isis.'
From the tale of *Osiris and Isis.*

37

Food and Feasts

Looking good

For feasts and festivals everyone wanted to look their best. Men who lived before the New Kingdom found this was easy – all they needed was a clean white kilt (the standard dress) tied at the waist. The wealthy might also slip into a pair of woven sandals. In later times, men wore a pleated skirt over their kilt and a sort of cape over their shoulders.

Women wore a full-length white dress. Some had shoulder straps. Like men's dress, women's clothes became more elaborate after about 1500 BC. Paintings show flowing pleated dresses with fringes, sometimes in stripes and other bright colours.

Queen Tiy (about 1390–1340 BC), the chief wife of King Amenhotep III and mother of King Akhenaten, the worshipper of the sun disc, Aten.

Wigs and kohl

For comfort and cleanliness, the Egyptians cut their hair short. On formal occasions the upper classes wore long, straight wigs. Kings wore special false beards, too.

Most men and women wore make-up. Kohl, a form of heavy eye-liner made from lead ore and oil, helped their eyes look good and protected them from the harsh desert climate. Lips and cheeks were coloured with red ochre. Yellow-orange henna was applied to fingernails and toenails.

Rings and things

The fine gold and turquoise collar that Atet put on for her banquet was typical of the heavy jewellery favoured by rich Egyptian men and women as a status symbol. The jewellery worn by most people of her class, male and female, was made from gold and silver. It was decorated with

Festivals and Feasts

semi-precious stones and minerals, such as amethyst and onyx. Poorer people wore copper and bronze jewellery, or even just strings of shells.

Like today, the most common forms of jewellery were rings, earrings, necklaces and bracelets. Armlets and anklets were also popular. Special pieces of jewellery – amulets – served a double purpose. As well as looking good, they helped ward off evil spirits.

Jewellery from the pyramids. This golden collar belonged to Princess Neferuptah and was found in her pyramid.

'Anpu's wife was a beautiful girl with dark gleaming eyes and an elegant posture.'

From the New Kingdom tale *The Treacherous Wife*, written about 1200 BC.

Food and Feasts

Food and drink

Atet spared no expense to make her banquet an event to remember. The evidence of texts and paintings suggests that the ancient Egyptians were keen party-goers who knew how to enjoy themselves – a feast was known as a 'house of beer'! The host's job was to provide ample good quality food, drink and entertainment.

Servants bearing jugs of potent wine and beer made sure no guest's cup remained empty for long. The food was the finest available. As well as her pigeon, Atet served roast duck stuffed with herbs, grilled slices of pork and a fruit basket piled so high that it took two strong servants to carry it.

Wider importance

However much they ate, drank and made merry, the Egyptians never forgot that every feast had a wider, religious importance. One party is pictured with miniature coffins arranged behind the guests. These reminded them that they would enjoy an even better life in the next world if they behaved properly in this one!

Atet's feast was in honour of Hathor. So as well as feeding her guests, she presented food and drink to the goddess' temple. It was laid before Hathor's statue at dawn and cleared away by the priests in the evening. Because the offering was symbolic, the Egyptians did not mind that the goddess had not actually eaten the food.

Noble ladies at a feast wearing their finest collars and earrings. The one in the centre is passing a pomegranate, a popular delicacy, to the lady behind her.

Festivals and Feasts

This painting from a tomb at Thebes shows female musicians and dancers. They are wearing gold earrings, bangles and armlets, as well as wigs.

Singing and dancing into the night

The feast started with jugglers, acrobats and other entertainers getting the guests in a party mood. Then came male and female singers. Finally, when everyone was relaxed and enjoying themselves, in came the dancers, leaping and twisting to the bewitching sound of lute, harp and rhythmic drum. We don't know exactly what happened as the party went on into the night, but several guests probably did not feel at their best the following morning!

'When's the cup coming round to me?.'
Comment of a guest in a painting at a banquet.

'Pour me eighteen measures – I love it!'
A woman's order to a servant pouring drinks at a banquet.

A bowl painting showing a girl with a lute. Music played an important part in all Egyptian feasts and ceremonies.

Food and Feasts

6 Uncovering Ancient Egypt

By the eleventh century BC, there was trouble in Egypt. The kingdom was divided in two, with separate rulers in the area around the delta and in the Nile valley. When divisions appeared among the delta governments, the empire became a tempting target for foreign invaders. The final chapter of a remarkable history closed with the conquest of Egypt by Alexander the Great in 332 BC.

For centuries the majestic monuments were damaged by vandals and eroded by the elements. Happily, the European Renaissance sparked a new interest in the ancient world. This increased during the seventeenth and eighteenth centuries. Napoleon's invasion of Egypt (1798) and the discovery of the Rosetta Stone, inspired a fresh fascination for ancient Egypt which continues to this day.

Collectors and historians

Nineteenth-century amateurs and historians packed off hundreds of priceless Egyptian works of art to Western museums and private collections. Meanwhile, archaeologists began uncovering some of Egypt's remaining treasures. The highlight of this process was Howard Carter's discovery of the tomb of Tutankhamun in 1922.

In the 1950s and 1960s, archaeologists hurried to excavate sites in southern Egypt before they were flooded by the waters behind the new Aswan Dam. Much progress was made before the dam's completion in 1970. Since then, interest in ancient Egypt has grown year by year. And the more we learn, the greater is our admiration for its many and varied accomplishments.

A silver coin with the head of Alexander the Great, the king of Macedonia who became ruler of Egypt in 332 BC, and founded the Egyptian city of Alexandria the following year.

Uncovering Ancient Egypt

> 'Say this spell over an egg made of clay ... then, if something comes to the surface, throw the egg into the water.'
>
> From a spell for sailors to drive away crocodiles.

An impressive legacy

Egyptian architecture, especially high columns like those in the hall of Dagi's villa, influenced the style of building in ancient Greece. This in turn influenced other architectural styles over the last 600 years. Modern medicine traces its roots to the Egyptian doctors of Alexandria. Egyptian religion almost certainly affected Christianity, too. There is a striking similarity between images of Isis and Horus and the Virgin Mary and the infant Jesus.

From ancient Egypt comes our division of time. Egyptian astronomers devised the calendar of 365 days. They divided it into twelve months of 30 days, with five days spare. The 24-hour day is another of their legacies. And the water clock – another Egyptian invention – was the world's first timepiece.

The temple of Amun at Luxor, founded by Amenhotep III in the fourteenth century BC. It was enlarged by later kings, including the great Rameses II.

Food and Feasts

Archaeology and inscription
Scholars learn about the world of Peseshet and Atet from archaeology and writing (inscription). Archaeological remains range from small pieces of pottery to vast temples and pyramids.

Archaeology is an excellent source of information because, firstly, Egyptian's important buildings were made of long-lasting brick or stone rather than wood. Secondly, Egypt's hot, dry climate is perfect for the preservation of all materials. Thirdly, the everyday objects that Egyptians placed in graves were not tempting to thieves and so have remained in place for archaeologists to study.

We have many examples of the three types of Egyptian writing – hieroglyphic, hieratic and demotic. Some are carved on stone, others are on pieces of papyrus. Although hundreds of papyrus fragments remain, they are fragile and sometimes hard to interpret.

The secrets of the stone
In 1799, one of Napoleon's officers came across an interesting-looking stone set in a wall in Rosetta (Rashid), near Alexandria. It was carved with Greek, hieroglyphic and demotic writing. Shortly afterwards, the British captured the stone and sent it to the British Museum.

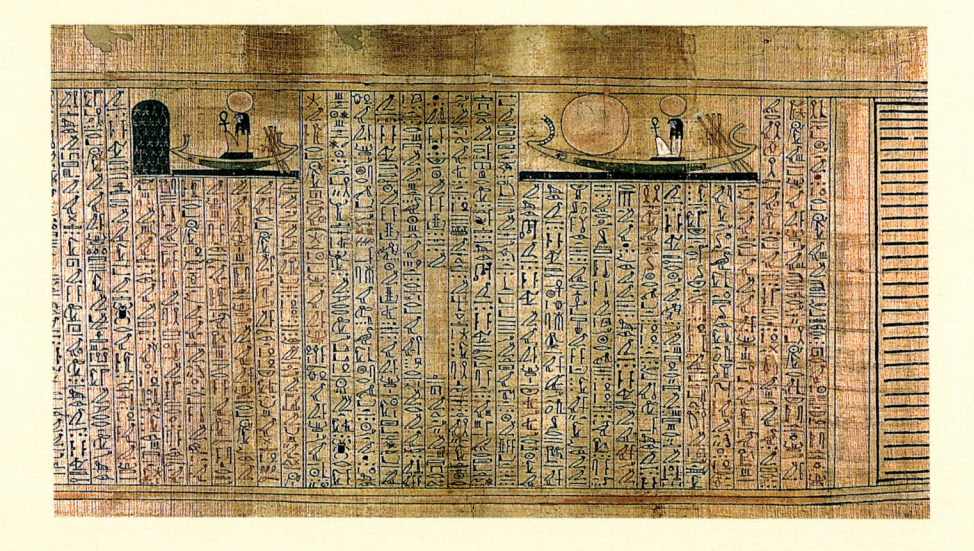

The mystery of hieroglyphics. This writing on papyrus is headed by images of Re as a falcon-headed god.

Uncovering Ancient Egypt

The French scholar Jean-François Champollion then worked out that the three types of writing were different versions of the same text. The hieroglyphs were a translation of the Greek. Using his knowledge of Greek he began slowly to translate the hieroglyphics. Thanks to this pioneering work, scholars were finally able to read the language of ancient Egypt and unravel more of the secrets of its magnificent civilization.

The puzzle of the past

Piecing together evidence about ancient Egypt is like reading a letter with the majority of the words missing. We use existing words to work out the missing ones. For example, could women like Atet read and write? Only a few notes written by women have survived so we cannot be sure how many women were literate.

Fixing exact dates is another headache. Egyptian lists of kings say how long a monarch reigned. But Egyptian years, unlike ours, depended on the moon. Moreover, they kept no continuous count of the years, so we don't know when each king reigned. But we can work out rough dates from references to the position of Sirius, the Dog Star.

'If anyone disturbs my tomb, a crocodile shall get him in the water and a snake shall get him on land.'
A curse carved on an Old Kingdom tomb.

The Rosetta Stone, the key to ancient Egypt. Discovered by accident, the famous stone had the same inscription in Greek, demotic and hieroglyphic. This enabled scholars to start deciphering the mysteries of ancient Egyptian writing.

Glossary

Amulet
Good luck charm. These were either representations of gods or goddesses (or their symbols), or hieroglyphs for words such as 'beauty' or 'life'.

Archaeologist
Someone who studies the past by examining physical remains, usually through excavation.

Bronze
Metal made by mixing copper and tin.

Caravan
Many merchants travelling together, usually on donkey, camel or horse.

Deity
Another word for god or goddess.

Delta
Where a river spreads into several channels as it nears the sea.

Drought
Time of no rainfall and severe water shortage.

Duty
Tax collected on goods coming into a country.

Dynasty
Ruling family.

Ebony
Hard, dark wood.

Empire
Several lands under the rule of an emperor, empress or pharaoh.

Ferment
Slow change or chemical reaction in a liquid to produce alcohol.

Hereditary
Passing on from one generation to the next.

Hieroglyph
Ancient Egyptian form of writing that used symbols rather than an alphabet.

Inscription
Short piece of writing, often carved in stone.

Kohl
Black eye-liner and eye shadow.

Nomarch
Royal officer in charge of a nome.

Nome
Province.

Papyrus
Tough river reed. The Egyptians made its stems into a type of paper, also called papyrus.

Pharaoh
Originally the king's 'great house'. Later, it was used to mean the person from the great house – the king himself.

Renaissance
Development of arts in Western Europe, from the late fourteenth century onwards, associated with renewed interest in ancient Greece and Rome.

Ritual
Important or significant action done regularly over and over again.

Semi-divine
Someone who is part god, part human.

Sickle
A farming tool with a curved blade used to cut or trim crops.

Tribute
A regular payment made by a conquered country to the country which now rules it.

Vizier
Important adviser in the king's household.

Time Line

All dates are BC and approximate only.

7000–5500	Neolithic Age.
5500–3150	Pre dynastic Period. Badarians settle in Upper Egypt. Hieroglyphic writing begins.
3150–2690	Archaic Period (Dynasties 1 & 2).
2690–2180	Old Kingdom (Dynasties 3–6). Sphinx and Great Pyramid at Giza built. Wars against Nubians and Libyans.
2180–2055	First Intermediate Period (Dynasties 7–10).
2055–1650	Middle Kingdom (Dynasties 11–14). King Mentuhotep reunites Egypt.
1650–1550	Second Intermediate Period (Dynasties 15–17). Horses introduced. Bronze used.
1550–1070	New Kingdom (Dynasties 18–20). Reigns of Hatshepsut, Thutmose III and Tutankhamun. Tombs built in the Valley of the Kings. Temple of Amenhotep III built at Luxor. Reigns of Rameses II and III.
1070–747	Third Intermediate Period (Dynasties 21–24). Conquest by Nubians.
747–332	Late Period (Dynasties 25–30). Conquest by Assyrians and Persians.
332–305	Macedonian Dynasty. Conquest by Alexander the Great.

Further Information

Books for children:
An Ancient Egyptian Child by J. Fletcher (Working White, 1999)
Ancient Egypt by K. Hayden (World Books, 1998)
Exploring Ancient Egypt by J. Malam (Evans, 1999)
Women in Ancient Egypt by F. Macdonald (Belitha Press, 1999)
A Visitor's Guide to Ancient Egypt by L. Sims (Usborne, 2000)
People Who Made History in Ancient Egypt by J. Shuter (Hodder Wayland, 2000)
The Ancient Egyptians by J. Shuter (Hodder Wayland, 1998)
The Awesome Egyptians by T. Deary (Scholastic, 1997)

Books for older readers:
Ancient Egypt edited by D. Silverman (Duncan Baird, 1997)
Atlas of Ancient Egypt by J. Baines and J. Malek (Facts on File, 1983)
Everyday Life in Egypt in the Days of Rameses the Great by P. Montet (University of Pennsylvania, 1998)
The British Museum of Ancient Egypt by S. Quirke and J. Spencer (Thames and Hudson, 1996)
The Egyptians by C. Aldred (Thames and Hudson, 1998)

Internet sites:
Browse with care! While there are some excellent sites on ancient Egypt, there are also some inaccurate ones. You may like to start with these.
http://www.guardians.net/egypt
http://www2.sptimes.com/egyptcredit.4.html
http://www.clpgh.org/cmnh/exhibits/egypt
http://www.ancientegypt.co.uk/menu.html

Places to visit:
The British Museum, London, UK, the Carnegie Museum of Natural History, Pittsburgh, USA and the Cairo Museum in Egypt, have excellent exhibits on ancient Egypt. A visit to the many sites in Egypt itself will give you a better insight into that country's spectacular past.

Index

Numbers in **bold** refer to pictures.

Abydos, festival of 36, 37
Alexander the Great 42, **42**
archaeology 42, 44

baking 26, **26**, 29
banquets (see feasts)
beer 27, 29, 40
boats 18, **18**, 21, **21**, 36
bread 16, **17,** 26, 27, **27**, 29
brewing **26**, 27, 29
butchers **26**

cereal crops 16, **16**, 19, 24, 25
clothes 6, 38, **40**
cooking oil 16
cooking utensils 29

dairy products 17, 25
diet 17, 25, 29
dining rooms 30

eating utensils 31
entertainment 6, 40, 41, **41**

farming 12, 13, 14, 15, **15**, 16, **16**
feasts 4, 5, **6**, 7, 11, 31, 33, 34, 40, **40**
festivals 32, 33, 34, 35, 36, 37, 38
Festival of the Beautiful Embrace 35
fish 13, 17, **24**, 25, 29
fishermen **13**
fruit 16, **17**, **24**, 25, 29, 40
furniture 31

gods and goddesses 9, 11, 32
   Amun 36
   Aten 32
   Bastet 37
   Bes 37
   Hapi 12
   Hathor 5, **5**, 11, 34, **34**, 35, 40
   Horus 34, 35, **35**, 37, **37**, 43
   Isis 36, 37, **37**, 43
   Osiris **11**, 12, 36, 37, **37**
   Re 9, 11, **32**
   Taweret 37
gold 19, 23, **23**

herbs and spices 16, 29, 40
hieroglyphics 44, **44**, 45, **45**
hunting **10**, 17

irrigation 14, **14**, 15

jewellery 7, **7**, 38, 39, **39**

Karnak 36, **36**
kings 8, 9, 10, 20, 21, 24
   Akhenaten 32
   Amenhotep III 8, 9, 43
   Tutankhamun 32, 42
kitchens 5, 28, 29

make-up 7, 38
meat 5, 17, **17**, 25, 29, 40
medicine 43
music 6, **32**, 41, **41**

Nile, river 10, 12, 13, **13**, 15, 25, 26, 27, 32, 33, 42
Nilometer **12**

nomarchs 5, 10, 18
nomes 10
offerings **5**, 11, **11**, 30
Opet, festival of **9**, 36

papyrus 13, **13**, 44, **44**
pharaohs (see kings)
population 11
pottery 13, **25**, 26, 29, **29**
preserving food 25
priests **11**
pyramids 33, **33**

queens
   Hatshepsut 20
   Nefertari **5**

religion 11, 32, 34, 43
rope-stretchers 15, **15**
Rosetta Stone 42, 44, 45, **45**

scribes 10, **10**
servants 4, **4**, 5, 6, **6**, 7, 23, 24, 29, 40
slaves 21, 23

taxation 14, 21, 24
temple of Amun 20, **43**
temple of Hatshepsut **20**
trade 18, 19, 20, 21, 22, 23

vegetables 16, 25, 29
viziers 10

water 26, 27
wine 16, 18, 19, 28, **28**, 40
wood 18, 28